Hot Chocolate With God 3

Hot Chocolate With God 3

Just Me & the God Who Loves Me

Camryn Kelly

with Jill and Erin Kelly

FaithWords

New York   Boston   Nashville

All Scripture quotations, unless otherwise indicated, are taken from THE HOLY BIBLE, NEW INTERNATIONAL VERSION®. NIV®. Copyright © 1973, 1978, 1984 by Biblica, Inc™. Used by permission of Zondervan. All rights reserved.

Scripture quotations marked The Message are taken from The Message. Copyright © 1993, 1994, 1995, 1996, 2000, 2001, 2002 by NavPress Publishing Group. Used by permission. All rights reserved.

FaithWords
Hachette Book Group
237 Park Avenue
New York, NY 10017

www.faithwords.com

Printed in the United States of America

CWM

First Edition: September 2013
10 9 8 7 6 5 4 3 2 1

FaithWords is a division of Hachette Book Group, Inc.
The FaithWords name and logo are trademarks of Hachette Book Group, Inc.

The Hachette Speakers Bureau provides a wide range of authors for speaking events. To find out more, go to www.hachettespeakersbureau.com or call (866) 376-6591.

The publisher is not responsible for websites (or their content) that are not owned by the publisher.

Library of Congress Control Number: 2013941576

ISBN: 978-0-89296-842-8 (pbk.)

This very cool
book is dedicated
to an amazing,
incredible GOD,
and to all the girls
chosen by HIM; for
HIS great purpose
in this world!

This ONE-of-a-KIND book

belongs to the ONE and ONLY:

_____

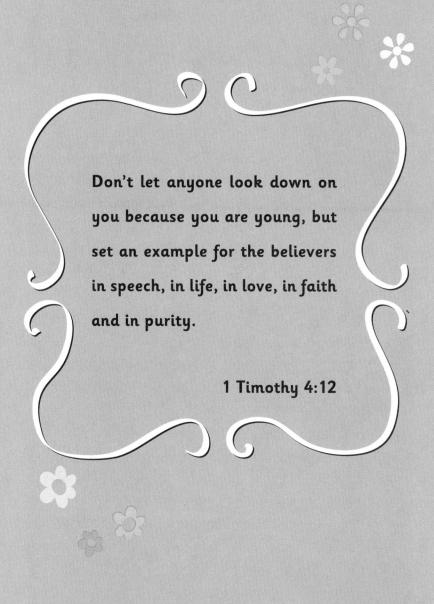

Don't let anyone look down on you because you are young, but set an example for the believers in speech, in life, in love, in faith and in purity.

1 Timothy 4:12

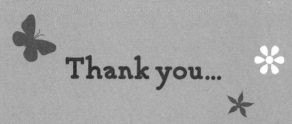

Thank you...

Ally Curtin—You're absolutely, without a doubt, the funniest person I know. Thank you for all you have done to help make this book rock! You're my BFF, and I love you!

Kim and Paige Waggoner—Aunt Kim and Paige, thank you for praying and for helping **HCWG #3** be the very best it can be! Love you so much!

Rick Kern—Thank you for your friendship and for always being there to edit everything **Hot Chocolate**. You're actually very funny! God has blessed us through you.

The FaithWords team—Jana, we love you and thank God for you. Thank you for helping us to make everything **Hot Chocolate With God**—great! Go Bills and Titans, and go **HCWG**!

Team Wolgemuth—Thank you for supporting our family. We are so grateful for all of you.

A special thank-you—To all of our friends who helped make the great **Cam Clips**: Pastor Gold, Mrs. Basinski—oh, and Daddy and Grammie—we love you!

To my mom and sister, Erin—I love you more! Here we are again, and it's great because God is so good to allow us to do this together. Talk about making memories. ☺

Finally, to Jesus—Thank you for loving me and for allowing me the honor and privilege of sharing how amazing YOU are with girls through **HCWG**. Everything we do **is for YOU**. Please help us to BE an EXAMPLE—in speech, life, love, faith, and purity!

Contents

Let's Get This PARTY Started...

Okay, so how can this book be a party? Good question! And here's the answer—this is not just a book. If you've already read **HCWG #1** and **#2** (**Hot Chocolate With God—Just Me & Who God Created Me to Be** and **Hot Chocolate With God #2—Just Me & My Friends and Family**), you know there's nothing ordinary about the book you're holding right now.

This book is more than a diary. It's more than a journal.

It's *you*!

It's your story.

Your life.

Your moments.

Your party. Yes, I know you're probably still wondering where the "party" is in all of this, so let me explain. Think about it this way— when you were born, everything changed. You changed the world just by being born, by being you. The "you" that **God** chose to create is like no one else in the entire world. That's something to celebrate. Therefore, this is a party—a celebration in honor of you and the out-of-this-world **GOD** who created you.

Are you with me?

How cool would it be if we could actually hang out—you know, like in person, face to face? Just think, if we never meet this side of eternity, heaven is right around the corner, and we will absolutely be together there someday.

I can just see us now, hanging out with Jesus and laughing till our sides hurt as He tells us how He was going for "cute" so He made the rabbit a fuzzy little chunkster with a fluffy ball for a tail. We're all laughing so hard the tears are running down our cheeks as He explains how He gave the bunny "hops" but realized that it would never be able to hop out of harm's way—so He figured He'd make it speedy!

The Lord's laughter is contagious as He shares how funny it was to see the little fuzzball hopping like crazy. We're all hysterical as He continues to talk about the first time He saw this little white blur go whipping by. His eyes twinkle as He tells us more about creating all the animals.

Can you even imagine? Girl, we have so much to look forward to!

Until that day, here we are...

Since the writing of **HCWG #2** so much has happened. First of all, I'm a TEENAGER now! WHAT? Um, yes, it's true. I'm thirteen! So I suppose you could say I'm not only older but I'm certainly much wiser than I used to be (at least I sure hope I am). It's sort of weird that I'm no longer a "tween," but it happens to all of us, right? We all get older.

Because I'm older, I have even more to share with you this time. More girl talk and maybe a little boy talk too. More

Cam Clip videos and **Sweet Truths**. (If you don't know what these are, keep reading because I'll explain in a minute.) More sharing of the real stuff in life that we all go through.

But better than all that, **HCWG #3** is about **GOD**!

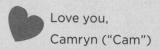 The One who loves you more than you can imagine, beyond what you can dream or comprehend. He's the superstar, hero, rock star of this party, and we're going to find out why.

Are you ready for this?

Do you think you're up for it?

If you know me, you know that I'm with you. I'll be praying and laughing right along with you, every step of the way.

Sooo...let's get this **PARTY** started!

Love you,
Camryn ("Cam")

YOU Absolutely MUST READ THIS...I'm Serious!

If you're reading this right now, I'm so proud of you. You might already be familiar with the way we do things in the **HCWG** world, and that's very cool because this will all make sense to you. If you're new to **Hot Chocolate With God**, **KEEP READING!** It's very important that you know a few things before we party on.

1. The **PRIVACY POLICY**! What you write here—stays here. This is your space to share how you feel and say what you want. A place to be **YOU**!

2. In case you haven't figured it out yet, I go by my nickname, Cam. I've decided to join this party, so you'll find **Cam Jam** here and there as you read. This is where I share my heart and life and sometimes goofy things with you. I'm me, and I hope that talking about anything and everything with you will encourage you to do the same. Besides, girl, God made you. He has an incredible plan for your life! So let's celebrate together.

3. We have a website! YES! Thank the LORD! Throughout this journey I will invite (or lovingly insist) you go to the **Hot Chocolate With God** website (www.hotchocolatewithgod.com) to view **Cam Clips**. When you see a **Cam Clip**, there will be a special code word next to it. At the **Cam**

Clip section of the website you will type in these special codes to view the fun videos. No one can view these videos without typing in the code exactly as you see it in the book. In other words—our **HCWG** GIRLS (the chicas reading this book, like you) are the only people who get to watch these videos. **COOL!** Yeah, I know. ☺ And there are more cool clips in this book than in any of our other books. Oh yeah, rockin' the videos this time around.

IMPORTANT! DO NOT FORGET to ask your parents before you get on the Internet. There's a lot of junk out there, and it's super important to protect your eyes and ears from what can harm your heart. So MAKE SURE you ask your parents!

4. During your **HCWG #3** adventure, you will read **Sweet Truths.** These are awesome, incredible words from God's book—the Bible. If you've never read the Bible, that's totally okay. God reveals Himself and His heart through Creation and His Son, Jesus, and He talks to us through His Word and prayer. You'll see!

5. Last, *you* are a gift to this world! Created by God and for Him, to be exactly...well, *you*! As you continue to grow (to become a teenager like me—oh yeah!) and learn more about the God who loves you—*you go, girl!* Go and take this party to the world. Go and SHARE YOU! Go and SHARE GOD! Wherever you are, go and share *all* that *you* are! God is with you every minute of every step of the way! ☺

Sweet Section

1

The Celebration of You

*G*o back to the party…

Before we get on with it, I think I need to remind you of something I said earlier. Yes, I know, but it's worth repeating: *This book is more than a diary. It's more than a journal. It's you. It's your story. Your life. Your moments. Your party. Think about it this way: When you were born, everything changed. You changed the world just by being born, by being you. The "you" that God chose to create is like no one else in the entire world. That's something to celebrate. Therefore, this is a party…a celebration in honor of you and the out-of-this-world GOD who created you.*

That's it!

What?

Your party!

The celebration of YOU, girl!

Okay, so I'm sort of confused now too. Just kidding. I know exactly where I'm going with all this. Let's get one thing crystal clear right now, okay? GOD created you! Yes, He chose to involve your mother and father in this amazing process, but the bottom line is this: You are here—living, breathing, and being you—all because God wanted you to be born. All because He determined long ago (and I don't mean like a few hundred years ago, I mean like way before time began—and who can understand

that?) that on a specific day at a certain time, you would be born. So tell me, what's your birthday? _____
(Mine is June 24, 1999—yup, I'm a summer baby.)

It's not by chance that you're here. What is "chance" anyway? Sheesh! It's not like aliens (as if they even exist) brought you to earth—although sometimes when I see my mother in the morning before she's had her coffee I can't help but wonder (just kidding, Mom). And come on, do people seriously think that we "evolved" from monkeys? (I suppose we sometimes act ridiculous enough that we might be mistaken for animals—but what a joke. Humans are humans. Animals are animals.)

God wanted to express Himself in a mighty, over-the-top way. He wanted to show off and display to the watching world that He is awesome!

Therefore...

He...

Created...

Y-O-U!

This is outrageously amazing! Why? Because no one else can celebrate the gift of your life like you can. No one can tell the story of what God is doing in and through you...but you.

Listen, my friend—if you understand what I'm trying to say right now, it will change your life. It will **CHANGE YOUR LIFE!** (Sorry, I just had to **SHOUT IT!**) How? Well, if you let this all sink into your heart, you will overflow with joy. You will want to celebrate! And that's where the party starts!

It all starts with knowing and believing that YOU are God's idea! And because you're His, everything about your life is a celebration.

I know, I know, you're thinking about the times when you've cried your eyes out until you had no more tears left—the moments that hurt so badly you wished you could run far away and never come back.

How can life be a celebration when so many bad things happen?

That's a good question. And believe me, I'm not "SuperCam"—the girl with all the answers. I've probably asked all the same frustrating questions that you have. I don't know all the answers. (My mom and dad don't know all the answers either. Sometimes I think my dog, Bella, has answers that seem to make more sense than a lot of people—ha-ha-ha—but even she doesn't know everything.)

Yeah, some of the questions we have might not ever be answered until we get to heaven. (Ouch, sure wish God didn't make us wait.)

God knows!

And sometimes, knowing that He knows has to be enough. We all have a choice—will we walk by faith, trusting Him with everything, including what we don't know and understand? Or will we stumble through the doubt, fearful because of those things we don't know? For me, I don't have to know as long as I know He knows!

I'm sort of getting deep, right?

Back to the party...

Because God made you...

You are beautifully and wonderfully made. **NOTHING** about you is a mistake because **GOD** *never* makes mistakes!

Celebrate!

It's time...

It's time to have the best time celebrating you!

Life as you know it is about to change!

Oh, and for those of you who don't like change— CHANGE is GOOD!

Why?

Well, because God never changes! He is the same yesterday, today, and forever. And because He never changes, you can trust Him when things in your life change.

What a relief!

Let's go!

Fifty-Three Must-Answer Questions—and Everything Else

Um, I know you just said to yourself, "Why fifty-three?" And the answer is—I have no idea! Okay, on to the questions, all fifty-three of them!

1. What's the date today, and how old are you?

2. Right where you are, write down the first **four things** that you see:

1.

2.

3.

4.

3. Okay, let's just get this very important question out of the way right now. Have you ever stepped in dog poop? (GROSS!)

4. I'm still laughing, are you? Speaking of laughter, please share a story or joke or whatever that you think would crack me up. Or maybe it's a weird face or break-dancing that gets you cracking up. Oh wait, how about talking in another language or with an accent? Whatever it is, share it.

Cam Jam: **You have to see and hear this. I can't even believe I'm actually going to do this. LOL! I'm not even going to tell you what this video is about. You'll just have to watch it.**

J **CAM CLIPS** CODE: LOL

5. Do you like your laugh? Which one of your family members has the best laugh? Which one of your friends has the best laugh? (It's like when these people laugh, their laugh makes you laugh.)

Cam Jam: **Some people say that laughter is "good medicine." Wouldn't it be so totally cool if you could actually take medicine that made you laugh? Oh boy, I'd be trying to get Mom to give that to me all the time.**

6. If you could create a medicine for something specific, what would you create and what would your medicine do for people?

7. Sometimes laughter and embarrassment go together. SOMETIMES. So I was just wondering, what was your most embarrassing moment ever? What made it so embarrassing?

8. Since we're kind of talking about "moments," what was the scariest moment in your life? Did the hair stand up on the back of your neck, and did you get chill bumps when it happened? What did you do?

9. What was the best moment you've ever experienced? (Life is made up of moments. Some good. Some not so good. Some we never forget. Some we wish we could forget. Tell me about your unforgettable MOMENT.)

10. And what about dreams? I've had some really weird dreams. How about you? Describe the strangest dream you've ever had.

11. Did your dream cause you to wake up? Were you able to get back to sleep? And did you go back to that same dream? Ha-ha-ha—sorry about all the questions.

12. Did you read the beginning of this book? Like the "YOU Absolutely MUST READ THIS" section? Be honest.

13. If you answered yes to the previous question, good for you! If you answered no, I have to ask, do you like to do things your way? In other words, are you good at listening and following directions?

Cam Jam: **Hey, here's a quick but very important reminder for you: NO ONE is perfect! We all make mistakes. But God is good. He loves us anyway. I'll tell you about that later.**

14. Please print your full name (including your nickname).

15. Okay, now this is going to be a bit tricky but really fun. Grab a marker (a cool color, of course), put the marker in your mouth, and write your full name using your mouth. How did it turn out?

16. Now close your eyes and write your name here. How did you do? You write your name so often that you probably did a pretty good job without looking.

17. Hair color? Eye color? Teeth color? (Ba-ha-ha, yeah, don't be afraid; we all have purple teeth. In fact, that should be the next big thing. Instead of coloring your hair, why not color your teeth? Mine would definitely be purple. Or maybe like a turquoise blue. SMILE ☺—say "cheese." Hmm, why do they tell you to say "cheese" for photos? Why not pizza, or pretzels, or peanut butter? Just asking!)

18. Since we're talking about teeth, do you still have some of your baby teeth? If you do, how many?

19. Do you like getting your teeth cleaned by the dentist? What flavor toothpaste do you usually choose? Does your dentist give you a new toothbrush and floss? Um...do you floss your teeth every day? (Ugh, I don't. I've got to get into this habit.)

20. Are your wisdom teeth coming in yet?

Cam Jam: **Quick comment. If we call them wisdom teeth, why in the world does the dentist usually insist on pulling them out? I'm pretty sure we're supposed to grow in wisdom, so don't we need our wisdom teeth? Just a thought!**

And this, my friend, inspires me to share a **Sweet Truth**.

Sweet Truth **If any of you lacks wisdom, he should ask God, who gives generously to all without finding fault, and it will be given to him. But when he asks, he must believe and not doubt, because he who doubts is like a wave of the sea, blown and tossed by the wind. That man should not think he will receive anything from the LORD.** —James 1:5-7

Erin: YIKES! I have to have my wisdom teeth pulled! We had to reschedule my appointment, so right now they're all still in my mouth, all four of them. They actually hurt, and I can sort of feel my other teeth kind of shifting around or moving. My mother had all of her wisdom teeth pulled. Um, she fainted when she got home after her appointment. Oops, no worries, though, my mom is just the fainting type. I'm sure you'll be just fine if you have to have your wisdom teeth pulled. Besides, God is with you. He'll make sure everything goes as planned. Hey, and don't forget to pray for wisdom because God wants to bless you with everything you need for life—and we all need more wisdom.

21. What's your definition of wisdom? Like if a baby tiger came up to you and asked you, "What's wisdom?" what would you say? (First of all, how cool would it be if a baby tiger could talk? No joke, I think animals will be able to talk in heaven. We shall see.)

Definition: wisdom –
noun\
1 a: accumulated philosophic or
scientific learning: knowledge
b: ability to discern inner qualities
and relationships: insight
c: good sense: judgment
d: generally accepted belief
2: a wise attitude, belief, or course
of action
3: the teachings of the ancient
wise men

22. Where are you right now? Like are you at home, in
the car? Who's home with you? Describe where you
are and what's happening around you.

23. The answers to these questions sometimes change. (At least they have for me over the years.) What's your favorite color? Number? Ice cream? Toilet paper? (Did I just ask you what your favorite toilet paper is? Oh boy!)

24. What's your favorite room color?

25. Do you own purple nail polish? _____ If your answer is yes, please use your nail polish to write your name in the yellow-and-pink flower on the next page. DO NOT use any other color. If you don't have purple, wait until you do or borrow some from a friend. WHY? Ummm, because purple is my favorite color right now, and you know it's the coolest ever. Besides, it goes great with yellow and pink. By the way, what is your favorite color of nail polish? We did a fun **Cam Clip** about nail polish; you should check it out. Oh, and have you ever had designs on your nails?

Cam Jam: **Oh my, I just thought about something. You'll have to wait until the nail polish dries before you go on to the next page of questions. Sooo...it's time for a snack. Really quick, before you go, what snack are you craving right now? I'm hoping there are some BBQ chips in the pantry or grapes in the refrigerator. Yummy!**

26. I asked you a few questions back what color your hair is. But I'm just curious, do you like getting your hair washed at the salon? And do you like when other people brush your hair? Oh, and what's your favorite hairstyle? And ONE more hair question— did you ever get your hair stuck in the blow-dryer? OUCH!

Cam Jam: **I think it would be really fun to show you some cool hairstyles. Are you familiar with the sock bun? Hopefully we'll be able to teach you some cool hair tricks so you and your friends can try them together. Let's go!**

CAM CLIPS CODE: HAIRSTYLES

Cam Jam: **Because we're talking about hair and for the sake of remembering, I think it's time you did something RADICAL, COOL, and possibly UNFORGETTABLE. I challenge you to be BRAVE and COURAGEOUS! You will need a steady hand and some serious skill. Are you ready? Okay, I'm like jumping out of my skin because this is such a great idea. I'm cracking up right now so bad that I might have to take a pee break. You're just going to have to watch the Cam Clip to find out why I'm so excited!**

CAM CLIPS CODE: NUMBERED

Wasn't that **SO MUCH FUN**?

And ya know what? The crazy thing is not so much what we did with our hair; the AWESOME and CRAZY thing is— GOD KNOWS EXACTLY HOW MANY HAIRS ARE ON YOUR HEAD RIGHT NOW!

HE IS OUT-OF-CONTROL AWESOME!

If He knows the number of hairs on your head, you can be sure that He knows all the other details about your life.

He **LOVES** you!

27. What's the first thing you think of when you see the WORD:

Red:

Butterfly:

Hope:

Rainbow:

Fruit:

Stinky:

28. Seriously, would you rather sit down on a cold seat or one that's been kept warm by someone else's bottom? (Or fanny or bum—or some of you might call that part of your body your butt. Whatever you call it, do you get the point?)

29. Have you ever said you liked something just because everyone else did?

30. What's your favorite song right now that you could listen to over and over again?

31. Can you play air guitar? How about any other "air" instruments?

32. Have you ever thought about starting an "air band" with your friends?

33. What would be your air band's name?

34. Name **three songs** you'd play:

1.

2.

3.

35. Do you like dancing?
Do you take dance lessons?
Do you get embarrassed dancing in front of people?
What's your absolutely favorite song to dance to?

36. **VERY IMPORTANT**: Do you like PB&J sandwiches? What kind of peanut butter and jelly does your family like?

Cam Jam: For my school lunch almost every single day, I eat peanut butter sandwiches. That's right, no jelly. And **NO CRUST**, please! Usually we buy Peter Pan peanut butter. My mom has tried to sneak in that organic-type stuff but my dad only likes the good old-fashioned kind.

HEY! I think you're just about ready for a *BLAST from the PAST*! For the final seventeen questions I've decided to pick the best questions from **HCWG #1** and **HCWG #2**. If you've already had the time of your life with our other two books, this will be like a stroll down memory lane—full of laughter. If this book is your first experience with everything **Hot Chocolate With God**, you're in for a treat.

And I was just thinking, as time goes by, people change. So the cool thing is maybe the first time you answered some of these your answer was something completely different from what your answer is now. Check it out!

37. If you could pick any place in the entire world, where would you want to live? Why there?

38. Favorite home-cooked meal?

39. What food or drink have you tried that you'll never EVER try again? (Eww, disgusting!)

40. Where do you usually shop for cool clothes?

41. Have you ever gone bowling? If you're a bowler, what's your best score?

42. What **two things** are you most afraid of?

1.

2.

43. What are the **top three important qualities** to look for in a BEST FRIEND?

1.

2.

3.

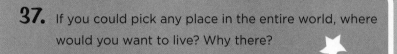
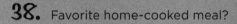
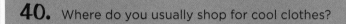
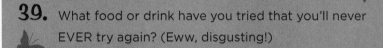

44. Write down **two words** that best describe your family.

    1.

    2.

45. What **three life lessons** would you share with a girl younger than you? In other words, what have you learned so far about life that you would want to share?

    1.

    2.

    3.

46. What grade are you in?

47. Where do you go to school, and who is your homeroom teacher?

48. If you have a locker, who has the locker to your right? Tell me at least one thing about this person.

49. What is your favorite subject? And what class do you dread going to?

50. Let's not pretend there isn't a cute boy in your class. What's his name? (Or maybe the cute one is in the grade ahead of you or possibly he's younger than you—do you have a problem with that? Please, do tell: WHAT is his name?)

Cam Jam: It's completely normal to think a boy is cute. Take Channing Tatum, TobyMac, and Justin Bieber, for example. Can you even imagine if they went to your school? NO WAY! Yes way! Let's imagine it for fun.

Write the names of **five celebrities** that you wish went to your school in the five stars. Oh, and I'm not a celebrity, but you can write Camryn Kelly in one of your stars ☺ if you have a blank one left over, ha-ha.

Sorry for getting sidetracked there. Now back to the fifty-three questions!

51. Okay, that was good. Now write down **three things** that come to your mind when you think of

_____ . (Write your name on that blank space and then get to writing.)

1.

2.

3.

52. What's your favorite season, and why do you like it better than the others?

53. And now, the last amazing, life-or-death, immense-and-intense, can-you-stand-the-suspense—final question of the Nifty Fifty-Three! Drumroll, please: *DO YOU LIKE HOT CHOCOLATE???*

The SOMETHINGS AND SOMEONES:

Tell me **eight SOMETHINGS** people don't know about YOU...

1. Something smelly:

2. Something that would make today the best day if it happened:

3. Something in your bedroom:

4. Something in your secret hiding place:

5. Something you like to do with your friends:

6. Something you wish you could do but don't know how:

7. Something you would change right now if you could:

8. Something that's really bothering you right now:

Oh come on, just a few more **SOMETHINGS**:

Something you've being hoping and praying for:

Something you like to eat that's sweet:

Leave it to me to add something *sweet*. ☺
So let's have some more fun with this! Instead of
SOMETHING, let's go with **SOMEONE**.

Cam Jam: **Wait a minute! Really quick before
we move on. IT'S TIME—go outside, or in the
basement or attic, grab a pillow or whatever, and
just go ahead and do it. SCREAM! As loud as you
can, for as long as you need to—just get it out, girl.
Because seriously, we all need a good scream
every once in a while. Right?**

Let's talk about that **SPECIAL SOMEONE**:

Someone you accidentally spit on while you were talking:

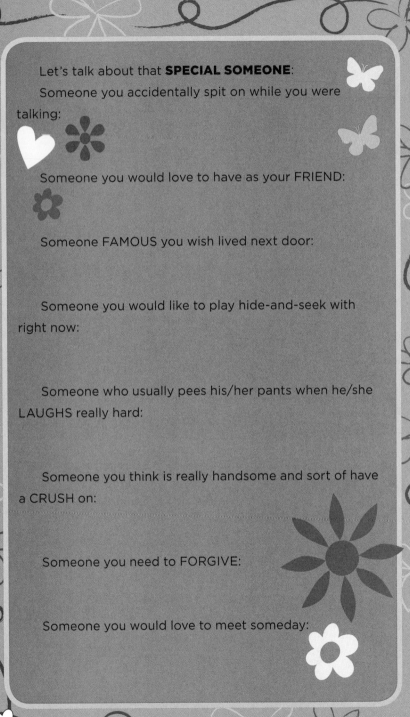

Someone you would love to have as your FRIEND:

Someone FAMOUS you wish lived next door:

Someone you would like to play hide-and-seek with right now:

Someone who usually pees his/her pants when he/she LAUGHS really hard:

Someone you think is really handsome and sort of have a CRUSH on:

Someone you need to FORGIVE:

Someone you would love to meet someday:

Someone you can't imagine living without:

Someone you know would be there for you no matter what:

Someone you need to PRAY for:

Someone who is ALWAYS there for you:

Major Cam Jam: **Like I said before, it all starts with knowing and believing that YOU are God's idea! So the next time somebody says, "Hey! What's the big idea?" Now you know— it's you, ha-ha-ha!**

So are you with me? This is a celebration of YOU! It's YOUR story from cover to cover, from beginning to end, and between every line!

No one else can fulfill the plan God has designed just for you; no one else has the dreams planted in their heart that God has planted in yours.

But don't worry; with God as the author, it's

going to be a real page-turner; a major best seller! (Unlike those schoolbooks you have to read—yikes! Please don't tell my teachers I just said that.) And like all good stories, there may be ups and downs,  and at times you might just about chew your nails off, but I confess: I cheated, I peeked, and I can tell you—it's got a happy ending. The Lord wouldn't have it any other way! His ultimate goal and joy is for His children to be together with Him, safe and happy.

So while we're waiting—whether we're stuck in traffic, trapped in an elevator (oh my goodness, that reminds me—I have to tell you my elevator story!), stranded on an island drinking coconut milk all day, or just super tired from a tough unit test in science class—let's celebrate!

Quick question: Have you ever tried coconut milk? _____ Did you like it?

Life is a breathtaking gift we should unwrap every morning, which reminds me of yet another **Sweet Truth**.

Yet this I call to mind and therefore I have hope: Because of the LORD's great love we are not consumed, for his compassions never fail. They are new every morning; great is your faithfulness.

—Lamentations 3:21-23

And this **Sweet Truth** leads me to wonder what compassion means. So—let's get a definition.

Definition: compassion – noun\ sympathetic consciousness of others' distress together with a desire to alleviate it

And all this talk reminds me to share one of the greatest **Cam Clips** I think we've ever done. SERIOUSLY! I'd like to show you some compassion in action. My sister, Erin, and her entire senior class went on a mission trip to the Dominican Republic. You must watch this video and witness God's compassion in action.

♪CAM CLIPS CODE: COMPASSION

Okay, back to the United States!

Hey, before we move on, what did you think about what Erin shared? Write down some things you learned from the video.

And I have to ask, have you ever been on a mission trip? If not, would you like to go on a mission trip someday? Where would you like to go?

When I move Bella (Hey, you might not even know who Bella is. She's our teacup Chihuahua. If you'd like to see her, she stars in most of our **Cam Clip** videos. Check 'em out!) out of the way, throw back the blankets, and climb out of bed each morning, I remember that the day is not the only thing that's new: God's compassions are new every morning too. Which means (at least from what I understand) that God understands me and He's ready to help me through the day. And because His compassions are new, life doesn't have to get old, even though I might be a day older—now that's *sweet*!

While God is doing what only God can do, I'm going to celebrate every heartbeat, every breath, every wonder, and every dream; trusting Him as I live the gift of life He has given to me—because...

Great is His faithfulness.

Erin: Awesome stuff here, Cam Bam—oh yeah, when Cam was little we all called her "Cam Bam" because in her newborn baby picture she looks like a little boxer (not the dog—a fighter). Suppa CUTE! Cam and I say "suppa" instead of "super" because, well, just because. Anyway, Cam—you forgot to tell them your elevator story.

Cam Jam: OH MY GOODNESS—that's right. Thanks, sissy. So we were in New York City a few years ago for my mother's book tour thing for her memoir *Without a Word*. (If you need to do some summer reading or chapter books for school, I highly suggest you read my mommy's book!) We were in this huge hotel and I was with my grammie and Erin. Well, the doors to the elevator opened and Grammie and Erin got off the elevator, but before I could get off, the doors CLOSED! As they were closing I could hear my grammie and Erin saying, "Don't worry, Cam, we'll find you." I was freaking out. I guess they knew I would be going to the next floor, because when the elevator stopped again my sister and grandmother were there for me. It all happened so fast. It's weird; when I think about it I get scared all over again. It's one of those bad memories I wish I could forget.

One QUICK QUESTION and an APOLOGY:

First of all, I just thought I would apologize for that really long **Cam Jam**! I had a lot to say—so sorry about that.

Also...

Do you sometimes have flashbacks from a bad experience that you wish you could forget? Tell me about it.

Now let's just pray about it! I'll get you started, but take some time to share your heart with God too. He's all ears! (Well, not literally! Ha-ha-ha!)

Dear Heavenly Father,

You know all things! You know what makes me happy and what makes me sad. You know when I'm afraid and when I'm mad. You know everything. There are some things that have happened to me that really bother me. I wish I could just forget about all of it, but I can't. But You can help me! Please remind me that no matter what You are always there for me—in the good times and bad. You'll never leave me.

This **Sweet Section** must not come to an end without a puzzle. Please take the challenge and see how long it takes you to complete it. Make sure you write down how long it took you. _____ _____

Time to Celebrate

```
R  A  V  M  L  K  Y  U  P  M  V  K
P  X  W  F  O  T  N  U  L  A  K  Y
Q  P  W  E  R  D  R  O  A  E  O  X
B  Z  Q  A  S  P  S  R  W  R  O  I
E  D  P  Y  O  O  Z  I  N  D  L  T
L  L  Y  S  C  H  M  L  W  A  Q  M
I  V  E  M  U  Q  S  E  W  S  Y  B
E  L  A  U  G  H  L  L  R  F  G  J
V  C  E  L  E  B  R  A  T  I  O  N
E  S  T  N  E  M  O  M  E  Y  D  V
B  V  F  H  E  A  H  J  D  R  S  A
Q  G  J  M  L  L  Y  G  Q  P  T  L
```

AWESOME	BELIEVE	CELEBRATION
DREAM	GOD	JOY
KNOW	LAUGH	MOMENTS
PARTY	PURPOSE	WISDOM

Sweet Section

2

My Life List: Love, Food, Heaven, and Skydiving

As you might have already noticed, I have a tendency to talk a lot—or write a lot. Come on, it's because I have so much to tell you, right?

I don't know.

It's weird because in person, like when I meet someone for the first time, I'm actually kind of shy. I guess you could say it takes me a little while to feel comfortable around people. What about you?

My BFF, Ally, is so friendly, funny, and outgoing. She can talk to anyone, and she's not afraid to meet new people.

Where am I going with this?

Ha-ha-ha-ha-ha-ha-ha...I have no idea.

I think I need a snack. I'll be right back. You can go grab something too if you don't already have some munchies with you.

Okay, that was quick. Hey, you never know when you might need some grapes and chips. Notice that I'm eating a healthy snack along with my BBQ munchies.

A growing girl's gotta do what she's got to do!

I think you're going to like this **Sweet Section**.

Here's the deal: I'm going to do my best to let you roll through this section with as few interruptions from me as possible. In other words—you're on your own, girl.

Yes, I'll still share my heart, but this is all you. Everything in parentheses is an official **Cam Jam**—okay?

Have fun!

See you at the end of this very, very **Sweet Section**.

Oops, I forgot to tell you what's next. First of all, you're going to need twelve different-colored pens. If you don't have that many, no problem, just use as many colors as you have. For each "list" I've provided five lines for you to write on. However, you might find that for some of these you have more to add: Go for it! Keep on listing wherever there is space.

This entire section will be called your **LIFE LIST**!

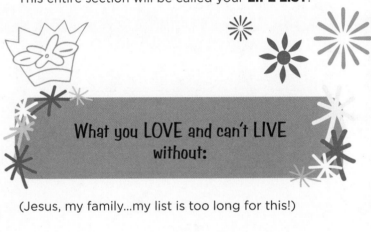

What you LOVE and can't LIVE without:

(Jesus, my family...my list is too long for this!)

_____

_____

_____

_____

_____

Things that ABSOLUTELY GROSS you out:

(Please...spiders, nose picking in public—eww! And what about when the person in the stall next to you in the public bathroom has a major gas problem?)

_____

_____

_____

_____

_____

PEOPLE you would like to MEET SOMEDAY: SUPERSTAR, NFL Quarterback, Olympian, Celebrity, Navy Hero?

(List all the people you would like to meet. Hmm, of course there are celebrities that I would like to meet, but I think it would also be cool to meet an Olympic medalist or a preacher like Billy Graham. He's kind of old, but my mom talks about how she would like to meet him, so I want to meet him too. Like mother, like daughter. ☺ And did you notice that I included an NFL quarterback—like my dad?)

_____

_____

_____

_____

_____

PEOPLE who have changed YOUR LIFE:

(These people have helped you to be who you are—one of mine would be my brother, Hunter.)

_____

_____

_____

_____

_____

Gotta-have-it **HCWG** GIRL LIST:

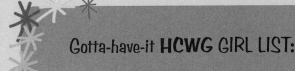

(These are all the things girls need! We are SO DIFFERENT from boys, aren't we? My momma says a girl always needs powder and lip gloss. I'm laughing! I'll have to have her tell you herself.)

CAM CLIPS CODE: GIRL LIST
WITH MOMMY

_____

_____

_____

_____

FUN THINGS you like TO DO:

(Hunting for night crawlers? UM, NO!)

_____

_____

_____

_____

_____

Official "TO DO" LIST:

(Like all the things you need to remember to do right now. Speaking of that, I better go start my homework.)

_____

_____

_____

_____

_____

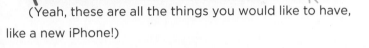

BIRTHDAY/CHRISTMAS/ VALENTINE'S DAY—ANY DAY:

(Yeah, these are all the things you would like to have, like a new iPhone!)

_____

_____

_____

_____

WISH LIST: "If I could, I would..."

(Find a cure for my brother's disease, skydive, and visit heaven.)

_____

_____

_____

_____

_____

FAVORITES—Foods, Songs, Animals, EVERYTHING:

(Couscous—yeah, if you don't know what that is, an adult will know!)

_____

_____

_____

_____

_____

PLACES you hope to VISIT someday:

(Italy...oh yes, you're on my bucket list!)

_____

_____

_____

_____

_____

NAME IT:

(Okay, this list must consist of things about you—things you like or dislike, your personality, and so on—that begin with the FIRST LETTER of your first and last names. For example, my name is Cam Kelly, so I would write down: C–Candy eater, Christ lover, Creative and for the letter K–Kickboxer—ha-ha-ha, just kidding—Kettle corn eater...this letter is kind of hard. Hmm.)

_____

_____

_____

_____

BEFORE HEAVEN:

(This is EVERYTHING you hope to do before you go to heaven!)

_____

_____

_____

_____

YOU—What people should know ABOUT YOU:

(I'm sensitive, and I cry easily.)

 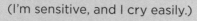

_____

_____

_____

_____

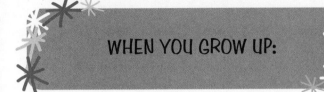

WHEN YOU GROW UP:

(All the things you hope to be, do, whatever, when you're old enough. A few of mine would be—own a husky dog and drive a Hummer!)

_____

_____

_____

_____

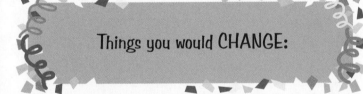

Things you would CHANGE:

(List what you would change about yourself, your family, and the world.)

_____

_____

_____

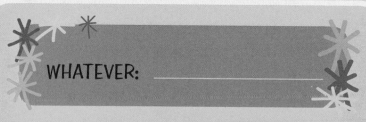

WHATEVER: _____

(You decide what this list should be. Fill in the blank.)

_____

_____

_____

_____

_____

Cam Jam: I'm hoping you had some fun "life listing." I didn't want to take up too much space in this book with some of my answers, so I decided to share them in a **Cam Clip**. I also thought it would be great to hear from Erin and a few other surprise guests. Check it out!

CAM CLIPS CODE: LIFE LIST

Sweet Section

3

The God
Who Loves You
Like Crazy

*L*et's be honest here, we've talked a lot about you (and me) so far in this book.

Right?

Well, I think it's time we focused on the **SUPERSTAR**, the **FAMOUS ONE**!

Let's talk about God!

Who is He?

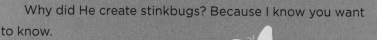

What is He like?

Why did He create stinkbugs? Because I know you want to know.

So let's talk about Him...

Talking about Him will no doubt be way exciting.

But before we get started, I think it's time for us to break for prayer. Ya see, whenever it comes to God, we are totally out of our league, if you know what I mean. And yet, God the Son, Jesus, calls us "friends." I know, it's crazy, isn't it—that the Creator of all calls us "friend."

Check out this **Sweet Truth**.

Sweet Truth

Greater love has no one than this, that he lay down his life for his friends.

—John 15:13

Since we're talking about "friends," I just had a few really easy questions for you before we move on to all the **AMAZING GOD** stuff.

First, tell me **three ways** in which you think Jesus is your friend:

1.

2.

3.

Maybe you're just discovering this incredible news for the very first time (that Jesus calls you "friend"). What do you want to tell Him right now? Like, it's kind of weird, right? But use your imagination and heart, and tell Jesus **two things** you want Him to know:

1.

2.

This is sort of a harder question—what I mean is, it might take some extra use of your smart brain. Say one of your friends is talking to you, and somehow you start talking about God and you know she doesn't know Him at all. How would you tell your friend about the fact that Jesus is your friend?

Okay, so are you getting aggravated with me because I'm not asking all easy-peasy questions? God did bless you with a brain so you would use it to the fullest. Wait a minute—I think it's time for a "nose check." I feel like there might be some boogies trying to dance right now. I'll be right back.

Yes, in case you don't know what the "nose check" is, it is what it sounds like: getting in front of a mirror and checking inside your nose. Gross! But, girlfriend, this is a must. And you need to check for your BFF too. We're all in this girl world together—right?

Speaking of nose checking with your BFF...
Who is your best friend?

Tell me **two things** you love most about him or her:

1.

2.

Okay, are you ready for this?
*Hello, GOD...here we come! Your **HCWG** girls are ready to dive in as long as YOU are there to catch us!*

Six—Yeah, Six—Rockin' Things God Says About Himself:

HOLD ON A MINUTE...
Before you go any further, I just want to let you know that this **Sweet Section** is full of **Sweet Truths**—more than any other section. So get your "sweet" swag on and let's go!

1. He is PERFECT.

Sweet Truth

Be perfect, therefore, as your heavenly Father is perfect.
—Matthew 5:48

What do you think it means to be "perfect"?

Humans can't be perfect—right? In fact, if I'm not mistaken, that's why we need a Savior, because we can't be perfect.

But Jesus commanded us to "Be perfect!" And not only did He command us to be perfect, just in case we didn't get it the first time (that would be me—not always "getting it" the first time), He said loud and clear, "...as your heavenly Father is perfect."

What's with that?

Why would Jesus command us to do something we couldn't do?

Whenever I see something like this I feel the need—the need to scream—or read! And in reading the whole conversation Jesus was having with His followers, I think we can better understand what He was trying to say.

Phew!

The perfection He was talking about had to do with loving all men like God loves them. He was explaining to them that they should love their enemies and even pray for those who cause trouble because that would set them apart as a child of God.

WHAT?

Love our enemies?

Pray for those who hurt us or cause us trouble?

QUESTION—We all know a troublemaker, right? And there are probably people in your life who have hurt you—maybe even on purpose. Let's talk about this for a minute. You don't have to share the name of the "troublemaker" or "enemy," but do share what happened.

Why would I ask you to do this? Well, it's important to talk about the things that hurt us. It's not good to keep things bottled up inside. In fact, I have a **FABULOUS IDEA**!

Let's do something really creative—a cool way to "bottle up" what's going on inside our hearts and minds. To do this you will need some supplies and instructions. In order to help you with this out-of-this-WORLD CREATIVE CAM project, you'll need to watch this **Cam Clip** to get more info! I'm pretty sure you're going to really enjoy this. Wait—enjoy? No, you're never going to forget it!

♩CAM CLIPS CODE: BOTTLE IT UP

WELL?

Did you "bottle it up"?

Erin: Hey, I was just wondering. We have fun thinking of ways to remember what God is trying to teach us. Maybe you have lots of cool ideas to share as well. Camryn and I would love to hear from you, so don't be shy— send us a message at the website.

God loves everyone—even those who want nothing to do with Him, and Jesus was saying that is how we can be perfect. We can't be sinless, but we can love like God loves—perfectly loving even those who don't love us.

So if you're like me—you're probably thinking, "Loving my enemy is so hard. How in the world am I supposed to love people that I sometimes feel like I hate?"

Do you feel this way too?

Since we're talking about love...

2. He is LOVE.

 **God is love.** —1 John 4:16b

This is love: not that we loved God, but that he loved us and sent his Son as an atoning sacrifice for our sins. —1 John 4:10

I'll admit it right now—there are a ton of things we could have listed here about God. We could write a billion books about all that He is. And of all the six things that we decided to share with you—this is my **FAVORITE. I LOVE THAT GOD IS LOVE.**

He doesn't just **LOVE** us—He *is* **LOVE**.

What does this all mean actually? What is your definition of **LOVE**? Fill in the heart on the next page with all that you think love is.

Love is . . .

Please fill in these two HEARTS of LOVE!

Whom do you love?

Who loves you?

God says He is love, but He also tells us what LOVE is—as far as His love. Check out this **Sweet Truth**.

Love is patient, love is kind. It does not envy, it does not boast, it is not proud. It is not rude, it is not self-seeking, it is not easily angered, it keeps no record of wrongs. Love does not delight in evil but rejoices with the truth. It always protects, always trusts, always hopes, always perseveres. Love never fails.
—1 Corinthians 13:4–8a

Wow—God is love!

Let's try this. It's Cam's paraphrase: Let's put the word "God" into the **Sweet Truth** wherever we read the word "love." And wherever you see the word "it" write "He."

Ready?

_____ is patient, _____ is kind. _____ does not envy, _____ does not boast, _____ is not proud. _____ is not rude, _____ is not self-seeking, _____ is not easily angered, _____ keeps no record of wrongs. _____ does not delight in evil but rejoices with the truth. _____ always protects,

always trusts, always hopes, always perseveres. _____

never fails.

This is **AWESOME**!
I especially **LOVE** that **GOD NEVER FAILS**!
What's your favorite part of this **Sweet Truth**? Is it that
God is patient? Or kind?

Remember the two **HEARTS OF LOVE** you filled in a
few pages back? Think about those people and write down
ways in which those people show you that they love you.
For example, one of the ways I know that my
mommy and daddy love me is because they
take care of me and pray for me.

And what about you?
Write down at least **three ways** in which
you show people that you love them.

1.

2.

3.

Cam Jam: **When you think about it, we can tell people we love them but showing them really makes our love real. In other words, our actions speak louder than our words. I think these Sweet Truths are a perfect example of what I'm talking about.**

Sweet Truth

This is how God showed his love among us: He sent his one and only Son into the world that we might live through him. —1 John 4:9

Sweet Truth

For God so loved the world that he gave his one and only Son that whoever believes in him shall not perish but have eternal life. —John 3:16

God *showed* us that He loves us by sending His Son, Jesus!

I think this calls for a **Cam Clip**. Let's ask a bunch of people what they think LOVE is. This should be interesting.

ꝯ CAM CLIPS CODE: LOVE

Let's talk more about your *heart*.

Your heart is full of so many things.

I'm sure there are things going on in your life right now that weigh heavy upon your heart. What do I mean by "weigh heavy"? Let me give you an example. My sister, Erin, is a senior in high school. She will be heading off to college soon. In fact, by the time you read this book, she will probably be away at college. She's more than my sister. She's my roommate and best friend.

I'm going to miss her so much, and this "weighs heavy" upon my heart. I want you to think about and write down in the enormous heart what is on your heart right now. For me, I would write these words inside the heart: "Missing Erin when she goes away to college."

When you're done filling in the heart, I want you to do a few things:

- On the back of the heart write your name and the date.

- Grab a pair of scissors and carefully cut the heart out of this book.

- Find an envelope, put your heart in it, and seal the envelope.

- On the front of the envelope, please write the following **Sweet Truth**: (Make sure you use a cool color pen.)

Trust in the LORD with all your heart and lean not on your own understanding; in all your ways acknowledge him and he will make your paths straight. —Proverbs 3:5-6

- Finally, find a special place to keep your envelope.

We've talked about God loving us and showing us how crazy in love with us He is, but what about us loving GOD? Before we even go there, I think we need to know this **Sweet Truth** first. (I warned you that this **Sweet Section** is overflowing, packed full of **Sweet Truths**!)

 **We love because he first loved us.** —1 John 4:19

So here's the deal—God loved us first! We can't understand or know what real LOVE is or how to love others and God until we get the fact that GOD LOVED US FIRST.

In what **two ways** can you show GOD that you love Him?

1.

2.

And here are some **Sweet Truths** that explain to us what love for God looks like:

 **This is love for God: to obey his commands. And his commands are not burdensome, for everyone born of God overcomes the world.** —1 John 5:3-4a

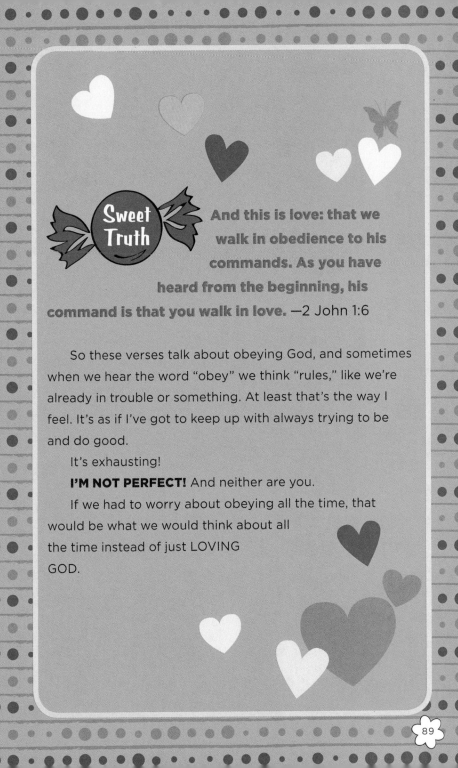

Sweet Truth

And this is love: that we walk in obedience to his commands. As you have heard from the beginning, his command is that you walk in love. —2 John 1:6

So these verses talk about obeying God, and sometimes when we hear the word "obey" we think "rules," like we're already in trouble or something. At least that's the way I feel. It's as if I've got to keep up with always trying to be and do good.

It's exhausting!

I'M NOT PERFECT! And neither are you.

If we had to worry about obeying all the time, that would be what we would think about all the time instead of just LOVING GOD.

Ya see, that's not what God is talking about. He's not up in heaven shaking His head when we make a mistake or don't do what we're told. God is cheering us on, and Jesus is even praying for us.

Quick Cam Jam: **Hey, listen—this is a lot of stuff to understand. I had help from my mom so I could tell you all this. We are all growing and still learning about everything—so just CHILL. God will help you to understand all of this. I promise!**

Hey, I was just thinking about something. Ya know what else is amazing? That even though God knows all of our mistakes, all of our problems, all of our nonsense—all of it— God still loves us!

WOW!

Just—oh my goodness—**WOW**!

3. He is ETERNAL.

Sweet Truth

Before the mountains were born or you brought forth the earth and the world, from everlasting to everlasting you are God. —Psalm 90:2

First of all—what time is it right now? It isn't hard to find out. Whether it's a wall clock, your watch, cell phone, laptop, desktop, stovetop, microwave, automobile, even television, there's a clock nearby telling you to set your life and move to its "ticking" (so to speak).

We live in time, and we're finite—limited—so it's hard for us to completely understand what it means to be eternal. To be forever—with no end over the horizon, and think in a way that's outside of time...Instead, as time passes, we do too. It changes us; we grow up and grow old, and age on and out—right out of this life and on to the next.

But for the sake of being an **HCWG** girl, what do you think it means that God is eternal?

If you could keep some things from this life for all eternity—meaning make them eternal—what **three things** would you choose?

 1.

2.

 3.

We all live each day in a matter of twenty-four hours. We determine and plan out our days based upon what time it is. Right?

Well, get this—God never pushes up the sleeve on His robe to check His watch. Even though we are "in" time, God is "out of" time. Huh? Wait, let me explain. We live by a set of hours, like twenty-four hours in a day, right? Well, God doesn't live in time; He is outside of time, not bound by it like we are. Am I making any sense here?

He doesn't need to keep an eye on the time.

He's never in a hurry.

He's never late or early—but **ALWAYS ON TIME**.

Are you always on time? Seriously!

When were you late for something that you wished you were early for?

Do you have any family members who are always late for family parties? Who?

Cam Jam: **Well, being on time just so happens to be a challenge for us. Now, when I say "us," my daddy would be the first to say, "Not me."—Ha-ha-ha. He's the "on-time enforcer" in our house. We live a thirty-minute drive from school and never know what the traffic will be like each day. My dad probably says, "Let's go, girls!" at least twenty times every morning to try to get us out the door on time— seriously. He would most likely say it was easier moving the football a hundred yards up the field against eleven huge guys than moving my sister and me ten feet from the front door to the car. Erin and I know that being on time is important, but sometimes we just can't help it.**

Erin: Cam, you know that we're late most of the time because of you. I'm not trying to start a sissy argument here, but let's be honest.

> *Cam Jam:* **Erin, are you serious? You know that even on the days when I was supposedly "late," the traffic was still bad. Hey, sorry about this. We're just being sisters!**

Speaking of sisters, here are a few quick **SISTER** questions:

First of all—do you have sisters? If you do, how many and what are their names and ages?

If you have more than one sister, where are you in the birth order?

Whom do you get along with the most?

Which sister sort of gets on your nerves from time to time?

Do you share clothes with each other?

Let me ask that last question in a different way. Do you sneak and wear your sister's clothes when you know she won't catch you?

What do you do together as sisters?

Cam Jam: **Erin is an amazing big sister. She really is. She's always willing to help me whenever I need her—especially with math homework. Erin and I share a room even though we each have our own bedroom. I guess we do this because we're sisters. We love each other. Now, just because we love each other so much doesn't mean we don't sometimes get really aggravated with each other. We have "morning attitude" from time to time (there's that word "time" again). What I mean by this is that some mornings we're both really tired and we're rushing around trying to get ready for school and we sort of tend to be rude to each other. But Erin always apologizes and then I do, and it's all good.**

Erin: I love you so much, Cam! I would do anything for you and always want what's best for you. Whenever I say anything to you that you sometimes don't like—stuff about your shorts being too short or whatever—I tell you because I love you.

Now, back to God being **ETERNAL**...

It's funny; you sort of can't try to understand eternity without thinking about time. For someone out of eternity (like you and me), it can be sort of confusing.

Also, over and over I have read in the Bible where we're told to "wait" upon the Lord. I can't help but wonder why waiting seems to be so important to God.

Tell me, are you waiting on something right now? What?

Oh boy, I should've added this to **Sweet Section 2**—but here it is:

Wait List

(List anything and everything you're waiting for. I suppose you could say I'm waiting to maybe someday have my own laptop and iPhone—did you read what I just wrote, Mommy?—but I'm also waiting to see my brother, Hunter, again someday in heaven. Hey, if you're not familiar with the story about my brother, you can check out this Cam Clip: (code) HUNTER. Hey, speaking of Cam Clips, I'm also waiting to hear from you at the HCWG website. Hint! Hint!)

_____

_____

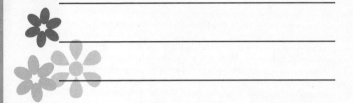

_____

_____

_____

There's no doubt that waiting can be really really hard. Like I miss my brother SO MUCH. And I know that God's timing is perfect, but waiting can be so long, it seems. Maybe while we wait God is strengthening our faith in Him. Like He doesn't just do what we want when we want Him to do it because He wants us to trust Him more...and waiting helps us to do that.

Are you waiting to see someone special in heaven? Who?

What do think you'll do when you see that special someone again for the first time?

Cam Jam: Oh my goodness, I cannot even imagine what it will be like when I see Hunter again. First of all, I'll probably squeeze him as tight as I can and kiss and hug him like crazy. I can't wait to talk to him and hear his voice because when he was here he never spoke a single word. I don't even know what his cute voice sounds like. But someday I will hear that boy talk. AWESOME! Oh, and I would really like to go horseback riding with my brother. He loved horses.

Erin: Wow! Just thinking about seeing Hunter again fills my heart. Sometimes I feel like I'll probably cry when I see him because I miss him so much. But we'll be in heaven, so my tears will be filled with joy, not sorrow. I don't know, just thinking about this overwhelms me.

Well, I'm glad that God understands all of this (and he understands me and you), and I hope He explains it to me in time...in time! There's time again—I guess it's everywhere, huh? We just can't get away from it.

So...let's answer some "time" questions...

Tell me about the last time you had the "time of your life":

What time do you have to get up and go to bed during the school year?

What about when you don't have school?

Listen, we're not going to start talking too much about school (just go with me here, girlfriend), but I was just wondering, how many hours do you spend there?

Tell me **two things** you really like about school. (At first I typed in "love," but then I thought for a moment and wasn't sure I could write down two things I love about school.)

1.

2.

Maybe you're homeschooled, like my cousins. I begged my mom to homeschool me but she was like, "Are you kidding me?" No, she didn't really say that. My parents actually thought about it, and Mom said she even prayed about it, but it didn't happen. She felt that God wanted me to be in school. Oh well. So if you're homeschooled, tell me all about it.

Homeschool Questions

 What time do you have to wake up for school, and how long is your school day?

What's your favorite subject?

Do you have to put book covers on your books?

Do you have a desk?

What **three things** do you do during homeschool that you would never get to do in regular school?

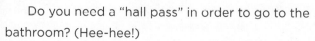

   1.

   2.

   3.

Do you need a "hall pass" in order to go to the bathroom? (Hee-hee!)

What's your absolute favorite thing about being homeschooled?

What do you miss about going to school?

Sorry for getting a bit off track. You should know me by now. I have a tendency to be all over the place.

Let's get back to talking about time. Do you wear a watch? _____ If you do, what does it look like?

This will be fun—take a quick break right now. Go walk around your house and count all the clocks. Don't forget to include the clock on your microwave and television cable box. Oh, and please feel free to grab a snack and drink while you're clock counting, unless of course you plan to eat dinner soon.

By the way, what time do you and your family usually eat dinner?

How many days during the week does your entire family sit down to have dinner together?

What's your most favorite home-cooked meal?

What's your least favorite home-cooked meal?

What food would you rather your dog eat instead of you forcing it down?

Do you drink milk with dinner?

Before you eat, who usually prays?

What does the prayer person usually say?

Cam Jam: **Wow, did you notice how easily I get off track? One minute we're talking about God and then the next we're talking about food. And I love both. Bah-ha-ha-ha...Well, here's the deal for Team Kelly: When Erin and I are busy with basketball season, it's a challenge for our family to have dinner together. This really bums me out. I love when we're together; we have a lot of fun sitting around the table talking and laughing. But the cool thing about all this stuff we've talked about is that since God is eternal and we will be with Him someday, we are eternal too. CRAZY! I don't fully understand this, but someday we won't have to worry about not getting to spend enough time together because we will have forever to be together. SO AMAZING AND COOL, AND I CAN'T WAIT!**

4. He is ALL-POWERFUL.

Sweet Truth

Who has ascended into heaven and descended? Who has gathered the wind in His fists? Who has wrapped the waters in His garment? Who has established all the ends of the earth? What is His name or His son's name? Surely you know! —Proverbs 30:4 (NASB)

It's not hard to think of God as being all-powerful—I mean, after all, He is God, and that's what God is, right?

Powerful!

Think about it. He parted the Red Sea so all Israel could cross it as if they were on dry land. And what about Noah's ark? Remember how he and his family found safety during the terrible flood? Wow, the fountains of the deep blasted open and it rained for forty days and nights.

I could go on and on...

Joshua led the people of Israel to march around the city of Jericho and give a mighty shout—down came its huge walls! And what about the teenage boy David when he picked out a smooth little stone from a river and that was it for the giant, Goliath, who had been making fun of Israel's army (and their God).

What about Jesus?

Jesus healed sick people, fed thousands of hungry followers with one little kid's lunch, He raised people from the dead—and then rose from the dead Himself.

I would say that it's obvious that God is all-powerful!

I love what Jesus said to His buddies one day while He was here on the earth. Check it out.

Sweet Truth

The disciples were even more amazed, and said to each other, "Who then can be saved?" Jesus looked at them and said, "With man this is impossible, but not with God; all things are possible with God."
—Mark 10:26-27

All things—and specifically you and me becoming children of the KING—are possible with God!

Yeah, and there's nothing in all creation that can ever be more powerful than God. He has power over everything that exists—in other words, God is all-powerful over all these things:

Nature: Nothing happens to the earth unless God says so.

By the way, what do you love most about nature?

People: He created all of us, and that means He knows what He's doing and has power over everything in our lives. Obviously, we are not puppets on a string. God allows us to make wrong choices, right? What I mean is that nothing happens in our lives that God has not allowed for a purpose—and we don't always understand this purpose, especially when something bad happens.

Tell me about something that happened that you didn't understand at first, but eventually God showed you and now you get it.

Wow, I was wondering—if God is all-loving and all-powerful, then why doesn't He come back and stop all the bad things in the world?

Good question, right?

I mean, why does He wait?

It's okay to ask these hard questions because God knows what we're thinking at all times, so why not talk to Him about everything?

In fact, let's talk to HIM right now.

What are some of the HARD questions you'd like to talk to God about?

Hey, now go and ask someone about what he or she would like to ask God? Maybe this person has the same questions that you do.

Now, take a few minutes and pray about all of this. Go ahead. Pray!

I found a **Sweet Truth** that has helped me understand why God waits instead of doing something right this minute. Here it is:

Sweet Truth

The LORD is not slow in keeping his promise, as some understand slowness. Instead he is patient with you, not wanting anyone to perish, but everyone to come to repentance. —2 Peter 3:9

So it turns out He holds off returning because He loves us all so much that He wants as many as possible to come to know Him.

I'll say it again: Wow!

How does it make you feel to know the Lord is willing to wait and let the bad things in the world continue because He's hoping that more people will surrender their lives to Him and live forever in His love?

Who do you know that needs to know the LOVE that God has for them?

And remember, while we wait for Him, its not like we're just sitting here watching the time tick on by, right? No, God gives us everything we need to live for Him each day. I've shared so many **Sweet Truths** with you, but there are tons more...more promises that God has made for you and me. They're all in the BIBLE.

5. He is ALL-KNOWING.

Sweet Truth

But when you give to the needy, do not let your left hand know what your right hand is doing, so that your giving may be in secret. Then your Father, who sees what is done in secret, will reward you. And when you pray, do not be like the hypocrites, for they love to pray standing in the synagogues and on the street corners to be seen by men. I tell you the truth, they have received their reward in full. But when you pray, go into your room, close the door and pray to your Father, who is unseen. Then your Father, who sees what is done in secret, will reward you.

—Matthew 6:3-6

I'm not sure why I'm going to talk about this first, but... I've got secrets.

I bet you do too. I guess we all do—it's normal. Some of them are nice things I've done that I don't want to brag about because that's not why you do nice things. Some of them are things friends and family have shared with me—because they trust me with them. That's pretty special. Sometimes they are things I pray about, for myself or other people.

Still other secrets stay hidden because I'm embarrassed about them. They're things I shouldn't have done, things I hope no one else ever finds out, or things I have shared with my mom or sister—maybe a close friend. Mostly those kinds of secrets are things I have shared with God and asked His forgiveness for. They stay between God and me.

It's nice to know that Jesus knows all about me—the good and the bad, and He loves me anyway.

He loves me because He made me...and because He's GOD and He is love—remember, we already talked about this.

This is all some really good news!

Listen, this is HUGE—we can be forgiven for everything we've ever done wrong, and everything we will ever do wrong!

God forgives us when we come to Him!

Since God is all-knowing, He has to know about our mistakes so He can forgive us for them—right? And He has to know the good we do and the ways we believe and obey Him to reward us—right?

Did you ever tell something to someone you really trusted—I mean a really important, private secret—only to have it get back to you that he or she shared it with someone else? How did it make you feel? What did this do to your friendship?

Was it hard to trust this person afterward?

When you know someone loves you, is it easier to share super personal things with him or her? Why or why not?

Cam Jam: **If you could think of one word to describe God, what would it be? The Bible has lots of them: the Prince of Peace, Sovereign Lord, the Almighty, the Lamb, the Lion of the Tribe of Judah, the Holy One, and on it goes....But there is one word that is used more than any other, in fact Jesus used it over and over and over again when He was talking about God. It is the one word that best describes Him more than any other. Any guesses? Father!**

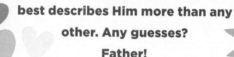

Sweet Truth

Do not be like them, for your Father knows what you need before you ask him.

—Matthew 6:8

That's pretty cool: Jesus speaks of this all-powerful, all-knowing, great big giant don't-mess-with-me God as my "Father."

He's my Father!

And He knows what I need even before I ask Him for it!

He doesn't walk around with a mean look on His face like He's ready to scream or like He's been sucking on lemons or something...

111

(Quick question in the middle of a thought: Have you ever eaten a raw lemon? _____ Okay, one more—have you ever made lemonade from real lemons? Like did you squeeze them and add sugar and everything? _____)

Sorry about that, I can get distracted easily.

Speaking of this—do you get distracted easily?

Oops, back to what we were talking about...

So there's this verse in the Bible in Zephaniah, and it describes God as a mighty warrior who delights in me and rejoices over me with singing!

Here it is:

Sweet Truth

The Lord your God is with you, he is mighty to save. He will take great delight in you, he will quiet you with his love, he will rejoice over you with singing.

—Zephaniah 3:17

Imagine that! Not only is He my Father, who knows what I need before I even ask for it, but when He thinks about me He begins to sing!

I wonder if He wrote a song titled "Camryn"?

Or if He lays awake thinking about how He's going to answer the prayers He knows I'm going to pray?

Maybe He smiles when He thinks about how I am going

to approach Him with my needs? Or maybe...He just starts singing!

If God asked you to write a song that you would sing over someone you LOVE, what would you write?

Take a minute or come back to this if you'd like to keep on moving. But DO come back and write your song.

Cam Jam: **By the way—who names their kid Zephaniah? Some of the Bible names are just so weird. I don't mean that in a bad way or with any disrespect at all. I'm just sayin'. Just a few quick questions about names before we move on.**

What's the most unusual name you've ever heard?

What's your favorite girl name?

What's your favorite boy name?

What's your pet snake's name? WHAT? (NO WAY—you don't have a pet snake, do you?)

What names have you thought about naming your children if you have them someday?

And...

This is a totally girl kind of a question, but here we go. Have you ever written your first name down with the last name of the boy you sort of like? SHH...I won't tell anyone. I promise! Write it here. Ha-ha-ha!

Are you thinking about whether or not you want to write it down? Oh, I hear you, girl. You never know who might snoop in on this book and read it, right? Yikes! Write at your own risk!

Before we move on, I just have to say a few more things about God being all-knowing. Hang with me here, this is a lot of info...but it's GOOD stuff we all need to know and remember. Here are some things that you might not realize that GOD KNOWS:

Your thoughts, actions, and words: Um, yeah, it's true.

O LORD, you have searched me and you know me. You know when I sit and when I rise; you perceive my thoughts from afar. You discern my going out and my lying down; you are familiar with all my ways. Before a word is on my tongue you know it completely, O LORD. —Psalm 139:1-4

Your needs and sorrows: Thank God He knows what we need, especially when we're sad and just need a hug.

Give your entire attention to what God is doing right now, and don't get worked up about what may or may not

happen tomorrow. God will help you deal with whatever hard things come up when the time comes. —Matthew 6:34, *The Message*

You know I could go on and on and on. Oh, and remember we already talked about the fact that God knows the hairs on your head. (In case you forgot, we talked about this in **Sweet Section 1**.) I just have to bust out with this: **GOD IS SO AMAZING!**

6. He is GOOD.

Sweet Truth

For the LORD is good and his love endures forever; his faithfulness continues through all generations. —Psalm 100:5

Sweet Truth I am the good shepherd. The good shepherd lays down his life for the sheep. —John 10:11 (By the way, that's Jesus speaking. ☺)

Sweet Truth The LORD is gracious and compassionate, slow to anger and rich in love. The LORD is good to all; he has compassion on all he has made. —Psalm 145:8-9

Cam Jam: Hey, just in case you forgot—which I do a lot—we learned what compassion is in Sweet Section 1.

God is just plain good!

Seriously, how else can we say it?

There are people all over the world who don't care about Him at all, but He still cares about them. He loves them even when they treat Him like an enemy—He still longs for their happiness and love.

Just think, God could say, "I've had enough!" He could

be like, "I'm over it!" Instead, He continues to patiently wait...
hoping people will come to Him through His Son.

> *Cam Jam:* **I think it's time to explain this to you in person. Maybe you don't know about what it means to come to the Father through Jesus. It's called "salvation" or being "saved." I don't speak all the "Christian" talk, but I do know how to share this, so come and we'll talk about it. Let's GO!**
>
> # ♪ CAM CLIPS CODE: JESUS

WELL...

What did you think about that **Cam Clip**?

Do you understand all of this a little more now?

Did you pray with us at the end?

And...

what are you thinking and feeling right now? Write it all down on this piece of journal paper.

Hi!

Okay, that was random!

But that's me. ☺

Just wanted to say a quick "hi," that's all.

And if you were here with me, I would hug you too.

Let's think for a minute about the way God teaches us to *be good* to others.

He said if you have two coats, give one to somebody who doesn't have a coat at all. (Do you call it a coat or a jacket? _____ Or a fleece, hoodie, or zip-up? _____ Um, what's a coat anyway? Just kidding!)

God also said if someone asks you to go a mile with him, go two miles. (Okay, truthfully, I'd have a hard time just going a mile—that's, like, too far to walk. Right? But He's not talking about actually walking. I think He's saying to be there for people when they need you most. Help others when they need you.)

By the way, have you ever walked a mile?

Do you know anyone who runs marathons and stuff? Who?

Basically, God wants us to treat others the way we want to be treated because that's how He is, and that's part of the key to our own happiness—being good to others! Selfish people who only think about themselves are the most unhappy people in the world.

Cam Jam: **There's no way around it; we're talking about good things but bad things happen to all of us. Some people look at their troubles and doubt God's goodness, and I guess I understand how they can feel that way—we've had some awful things happen in our family. But I kind of think that maybe looking at God through the things that happen to you make it easier to do that. We try to look at the things that happen through God instead. When we do, it's easier to see His goodness, or how He can use the things that happen for good.**

Sweet Truth

And we know that in all things God works for the good of those who love him, who have been called according to his purpose. —Romans 8:28

Can you think of **three good things** that have happened to you unexpectedly throughout your life?

1.

2.

3.

What about disappointments? Can you think of a time when you were deeply disappointed, but eventually it turned into something good?

Has anyone ever done something for you that was truly good, and yet there was absolutely nothing in it for them—it was just a selfless act of goodness?

If so, what was it, and how did it make you feel?

How about you—have you ever done something good for someone to make his or her life better? If so, how did it make you feel?

Random—write the first word that pops into your mind when you read the following words:

1. *Blessing*

2. *Frustration*

3. Hope

4. Disappointment

5. Good

6. Candy

7. Frogs

8. Jesus

I just had to get candy in there!
And God said it was GOOD...
I've been sitting here just wondering, what do you think?
Share **seven words** that describe what God is like, based on your personal experience and understanding of Him. Don't fudge this; give me what you've got. And if you don't want to honestly own this right now, then come back to it another time. No problem! Maybe your experience with God is but three words at this point—that's awesome!

Just be real and share, period!

1.

2.

3.

4.

5.

6.

7.

We're going to run through these pretty fast because we still have a lot to do together, so here we go.

Four Unusual Things You Might Not Know About God

1. His Hair Is White.

His head and hair were white like wool, as white as snow. —Revelation 1:14 (NKJV)

123

Who do you know who has white hair?

2. He Laughs.

Sweet Truth

The One enthroned in heaven laughs. —Psalm 2:4

Who do you know who absolutely has the best laugh?

3. He Sings.

This is a repeat but worth repeating.

Sweet Truth

The LORD your God is with you, he is mighty to save. He will take great delight in you, he will quiet you with his love, he will rejoice over you with singing.

—Zephaniah 3:17

Who do you know who can sing really well?

4. He Made a Donkey Talk.

Then the LORD opened the donkey's mouth, and she said to Balaam, "What have I done to you to make you beat me these three times?" —Numbers 22:28 (This story is really very interesting, so you should read it!)

Who do you know who talks like a donkey?

Bah-ha-ha!

I hope you've had as much fun as I have with this **Sweet Section**. Learning about God is awesome—and we will never stop learning about His greatness!

Let's end this section with another puzzle.

Once again, time yourself. See if it takes you less time to complete this one. Don't forget to write down how long it took you.

Ready?

Set?

Go!

The God who Loves You

R	J	F	U	U	R	L	L	M	H	L	J
S	O	P	A	E	X	I	X	O	E	A	E
Y	D	T	H	M	G	J	L	U	V	N	S
X	L	T	A	H	O	Y	K	W	O	R	U
K	A	O	T	E	S	U	W	K	L	E	S
F	I	R	H	P	R	G	S	X	K	T	F
R	Y	N	I	I	J	C	Z	H	R	E	U
T	J	R	U	M	O	L	G	H	A	N	P
R	I	N	G	I	E	R	E	V	O	S	W
T	K	B	I	W	K	B	H	J	O	J	R
P	P	A	N	W	T	B	C	G	I	B	Y
S	A	V	I	O	R	H	G	N	I	K	V

CREATOR	ETERNAL	FAMOUS
FATHER	HOLY	HOLYSPIRIT
JESUS	KING	LIGHT
LOVE	SAVIOR	SOVEREIGN

Sweet Section

4

Eternal Life List: God, Prayer, People, and Pandas

had such a great time with this in **Sweet Section 2** that I thought we could go for it again. I don't know about you, but I'm big on lists! I wonder if the Lord made lists when He was on earth back in the day? If He did, I sure wonder what He wrote them on—I kinda doubt they had spiral notebooks, journals, or composition books back then! Ha-ha-ha...and I know for sure they didn't have little sticky notes, computers, or iPads, right?

Hmm, I can just see it now:

THE LORD'S LIST FOR THE DAY

1. Wake up before dawn

2. Pray/have quiet time

3. Outline Sermon on the Mount

4. Talk to Peter about putting his foot in his mouth

5. Heal the sick

6. Feed the hungry

7. Take robe to the cleaners

8. Pick up sandals from shoemaker

9. Visit Mom

Ha-ha-ha, I guess I am a lot like Peter sometimes. I doubt Jesus had a list like that, but they sure are useful to me. Speaking of lists, use your imagination and dig crazy deep if you can. Come on, I know you're up for this. Don't get all formal or try to be spiritual (what does that even mean anyway?). Just be honest and have fun. If you do that, I think you'll take a step or two closer to Jesus. So be creative. Remember, God is the Creator, and He created creativity—so create!

First Words That Come to Mind When You Think about God:

(Jesus, hope, HUGE!)

_____

_____

_____

_____

_____

Favorite Things God Created:

(Dogs, BBQ chips, the ocean—girl, I could go on and on!)

_____

_____

_____

_____

_____

Questions You Would Like to Ask God about Himself:

(Of course, God is always listening and you can ask Him anything. But let's pretend He's snuggling with you on the couch and has offered to answer all of your questions. Here are a few questions I would ask Him: "Why can't I see You and actually hear You? Oh, and why are You waiting so long to send Jesus back to earth?" What would you ask Him?)

_____

_____

_____

_____

_____

_____

Amazing Things You Imagine You Might Do in Heaven:

(Meet Jesus, see my brother, EAT!)

_____

_____

_____

_____

_____

Official "Prayer List":

(Who needs prayer right now, and what do you need to talk to God about? For me, my list would start off with HELP ME, GOD! My sister, Erin, is going to college. She'll be far away, and I can't imagine her not being here with me. Okay, so I might start crying right now.)

_____

_____

_____

_____

_____

Thank You, LORD—for...:

(Yeah, we have SO MUCH to be thankful for! I would like to start off with my family for sure. I thank God for them! And I'm thankful for HOPE. Without the HOPE we have in God, we'd be in big trouble.)

_____

_____

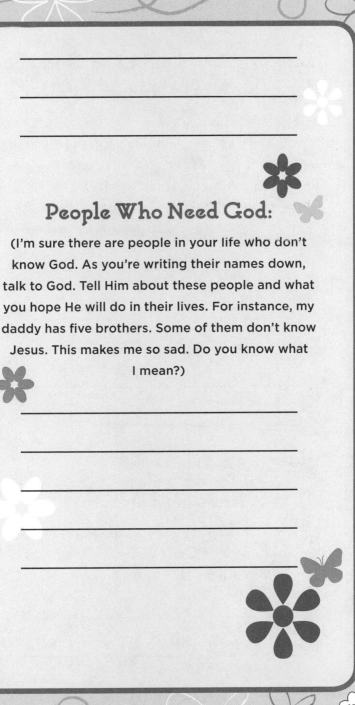

People Who Need God:

(I'm sure there are people in your life who don't know God. As you're writing their names down, talk to God. Tell Him about these people and what you hope He will do in their lives. For instance, my daddy has five brothers. Some of them don't know Jesus. This makes me so sad. Do you know what I mean?)

Questions You Would Ask God about the World He Created:

(Okay, I would absolutely ask Him these questions: "Why can't we have wild animals as pets? Like, if we can have dogs as pets, why not panda bears and tigers?" And "How come the ocean's waves only go so far? Seriously, how do they know when to stop and not keep going?")

_____

_____

_____

_____

_____

Answered Prayer:

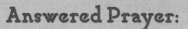

(Write down all the prayers you've prayed that God has answered. Don't forget to explain how He answered each prayer. I wish I could read yours!)

_____

_____

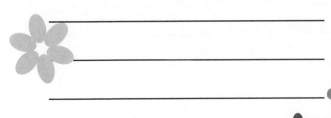

_____

_____

_____

Favorite Scriptures (Verses):

(Before you make a list—I just have to say that maybe you don't have any favorite verses. In fact, maybe you don't even have a Bible. It's totally no problem at all. Just leave this all blank until you have verses to share here. Actually I will put one of my favorite verses on the first line. I hope you like it. This is the verse that I use every time I sign an **HCWG** book.)

In his hand is the life of every creature and the breath of all mankind.
—Job 12:10

_____

_____

_____

_____

_____

Whatever: _____

(You decide what this GOD list should be. Fill in the blank.)

_____

_____

_____

_____

The Heart of God:

(What do you think would bring joy to God's heart? I'm thinking like maybe if I spend more time with God—yeah, maybe that would bring Him joy. Or what if I prayed for some people I don't usually pray for—like the people who drive me crazy.)

_____

_____

_____

_____

_____

_____

_____

Getting Radically Hysterical:

(List three things you think would make God laugh
so hard He'd have tears of joy in His eyes! I mean,
come on, He did make a donkey talk in the BIBLE.
He created humor and laughter. All good things
start with Him!)

_____

_____

_____

There Will Be a Day:

(Someday you're going to meet GOD face to face. CAN YOU EVEN BELIEVE IT? It's true! So what do you think it will be like? What do you think Jesus will be like when you see Him? What do you think you'll say to Him? I kind of wonder what heaven will smell like. I'm serious!)

_____

_____

_____

_____

_____

Favorite Christian Everything:

(I'm sure you have a favorite Christian song or book—at least I hope you do. If you don't, maybe you can see what mine are like. Right now, my favorite Christian song is "Me Without You" by TobyMac.)

_____

_____

_____

_____

_____

Who's My Neighbor:

(Write down a few things that you could do from home to reach out to people in other parts of the world or those who live right next door or around the corner from you. How can you make a difference in their lives?)

_____

_____

_____

_____

_____

Sweet Section

For the King and His Kingdom

Some things to think about and remember...

From the moment you were thought of in the mind and heart of God—He had a plan for your life. He created you!

When you became His child He gave you specific gifts so that you would shine for Him in this world.

Every child of God has been blessed with gifts but not all gifts are given to everyone.

God has very specifically created you to be you. And since no one else in the world can be you...you need to be you. You need to shine for Jesus with the amazing gifts that God has given you.

Your gifts are for Him!

They are to show the world how incredible He is.

God wants you to use the special gifts and talents He has given you. When you don't, everyone misses out on the great creativity of God through your life.

Your gifts are unique to you!

God knows you more than anyone else on the face of the earth—even more than your parents and brothers and sisters. You can trust that He has gifted you perfectly.

A great example of what we're talking about is your body.

Hmmm...

Your body is made up of various parts that all work together. The incredible parts of your amazing body must do what they are created to do in order for your body to function properly—the way God intended it to.

You have a nose, eyes, and mouth that make up your face. Imagine yourself as one big nose—ridiculous, right?

Can you just see it now?

Imagine if you had to sneeze! Whoa! Watch out, world!

Well, that's an example of why God has given different gifts to His children so we would all work together as a team.

The Kelly family is all about teamwork. Since my daddy was an NFL quarterback, he always says we need to do everything as a team. He's so cute! (Daddy love moment. ☺)

When we each share the gifts that God has given us with each other we act like a body—the body of Christ. When we do this we shine for God—and people take notice.

LISTEN—PLEASE HEAR ME—Don't be disappointed if your best friend has talents and gifts that are different from yours. Maybe she has a beautiful voice and you only sing to the shampoo and conditioner bottles in your shower. And may I remind you that you don't have to have a great voice to sound beautiful to GOD! Sing your heart out, girl! Maybe your BFF is the next Picasso and your best drawing is stick-figure people.

Bah-ha-ha—I'm laughing because I sing and draw anyway. In fact, I think stick-figure people are adorable.

My point is, instead of being jealous of each other or comparing ourselves to others and wanting to be someone we're not, we need to encourage each other to use the gifts and talents God has given each of us. We need to be thankful for what God has chosen to do in each of our lives.

God knew what He was doing when He created you!

You can trust that He made you exactly how He wanted you to be—with exactly the perfect gifts. And know this: No gift or talent is better than any other. Sometimes this is hard to understand because certain gifts seem to draw more attention than others. Right? Let's take me for an example. God has allowed my sister and me to write—like the book you're reading right now. This is a gift from Him that we are sharing with you. This is all God's work.

Your gifts and talents are His work!

He will give you opportunities to share what He is doing in your life. SOOO, be thankful and shine on!

WAIT A MINUTE...

I'm feeling a prayer bubbling up in my heart right now. COME ON! I'll get us started and you finish up. Okay?

Dear Heavenly Father...

Thank You for the gifts and talents You have given me. Help me to trust that You know what You're doing. Please help me to know that You will help me to discover and use the gifts You have given me. When I forget, help me to remember that Your ways are perfect and that I can trust You to guide me in every area of my life...

Hey, did you know that the Bible—God's amazing **LOVE** story—talks about spiritual gifts? Everything God wants us to know can be found in His Word.

Wait, did I ever tell you that I LOVE this thing called a concordance?

Oh my goodness, once again I'm laughing. If someone walked in the room right now and said, "Cam, what are you laughing about?" And I would respond, "Oh nothing, I'm just laughing about the concordance." Yeah, they would think I'm crazy for sure.

Instead of trying to explain what this is to you, I think I'll just show you. Let's go!

J CAM CLIPS CODE: CONCORDANCE

It's weird because I can't believe I actually really like my Bible concordance—hmm, God must be working in my heart for sure.

We were talking about spiritual gifts and the Bible, so here are some **Sweet Truths** to explain what I'm talking about.

We have different gifts, according to the grace given us. If a man's gift is prophesying, let him use it in proportion to his faith. If it is serving, let him serve; if it is teaching, let him teach; if it is encouraging, let him encourage; if it is contributing to the needs of others, let him give generously; if it is leadership, let him govern diligently; if it is showing mercy, let him do it cheerfully. —Romans 12:6-8

WOW...I'm pretty sure that was the longest **Sweet Truth** ever. But there's MORE!

 **Sweet Truth**

It was he who gave some to be apostles, some to be prophets, some to be evangelists, and some to be pastors and teachers, to prepare God's people for works of service, so that the body of Christ may be built up until we all reach unity in the faith and in the knowledge of the Son of God and become mature, attaining to the whole measure of the fullness of Christ. —Ephesians 4:11-13

And there's MORE...

 **Sweet Truth**

There are different kinds of gifts but the same Spirit... To one there is given through the Spirit the message of wisdom, to another the message of knowledge by means of the same Spirit, to another faith by the same Spirit, to another gifts of healing by that one Spirit, to another miraculous powers, to another prophecy, to another distinguishing between spirits, to another speaking in different kinds of tongues, and to still another the interpretation of tongues. All these are the work of one and the

same Spirit, and he gives them to each one, just as he determines. —1 Corinthians 12:4-11

Whoa, okay that last one was the longest **Sweet Truth** for sure. No doubt!

ARE YOU OVERWHELMED?

I am!

But all we really have to do is pray about it.

So let's pray again.

Like before, I'll get us started and you finish up—like team praying!

Dear Father...

Thank you so much for giving each of us spiritual gifts. Help us to remember that we have these gifts to glorify YOU and to build up YOUR KINGDOM. As we grow to know and love You more, please help us to know exactly what our spiritual gifts are. And help us to be faithful to use them...

If God took the time to explain these gifts in His Word, the Bible, He must have wanted us to understand and learn about them.

Right?

Write down a definition of what you think the following **spiritual gifts** are and how you would use them for God's glory and kingdom. If you're not sure how to answer some of these, think about who you might be able to ask for help. Of course my sister, Erin, and I are always here for you! We're just a message away—www.hotchocolatewithgod.com!

Encouragement

Faith

Evangelism

Giving

Hospitality

Leadership

Healing

Intercession/Prayer

 Pastor

Teaching

Showing Mercy

Serving/Helping

Cam Jam: **Listen, some of these I have no clue how to explain, so I think we should ask someone who might know. Don't you agree? Let's ask and learn. Maybe as you're watching this clip you can take notes. YAY! Write down what you want to remember next to the gifts we listed above. Great idea, CAM!**

CAM CLIPS CODE: GODS GIFTS

Here are some questions to help you start to discover and understand some of the **spiritual gifts** that the Lord has given to His people:

1. Do you like to get others involved in projects or games?

2. Do you like to create things with your hands—like art projects and unique creations?

3. Do you love to share your faith in Jesus?

4. Do you like to organize your room so everything is neat and orderly?

5. Do you like to plan parties and have people over to your house?

6. Do you pray a lot for other people?

7. Are you sensitive to the hurts of others?

8. Do you love to read God's Word and share what you have learned with other people?

9. Are you concerned that people don't know the Lord?

10. Is it easy for you to trust God for impossible things?

11. Do you enjoy music and drama as a way to share a story?

12. Would you rather be the one giving instructions or the person following them?

13. Do you take notice and want to help out when one of your friends is sad?

14. Do others ask you to pray for them because they know you will?

15. Are you comfortable sharing your faith with a new kid at school?

16. Do you think it's fun to study God's Word?

17. Do you think it's important to be there for one of your friends going through a difficult time?

18. Do you think it's important to work as a team?

19. Do you believe strongly that God is who He says He is and that He can do what He says He can do?

20. Do you enjoy working with paper, paint, wood, and other materials to construct things?

21. Do you long for all of your friends to know who Jesus is?

22. Do you think it's important to encourage your friends to increase their faith?

23. Do you help around the house and at school when you're not asked?

24. Do people usually want you to be the captain whenever you play group games?

25. Do you like to help your friends learn more about God?

Now, let's consider some other gifts. Write down ways in which the following can be considered gifts from God and how they can be used for Him:

1. Your personality

2. Your sense of humor

3. Your heritage (like who your family is and where you are from)

4. Your hopes and dreams

5. Your interests

6. Your talents

7. Your passions (what really gets you excited and fired up)

Regifting!

Have you ever done this before?

I suppose I should explain what regifting is first. It's when you've been given a gift instead of keeping it for yourself you decide to wrap it up and give it to someone else. (Sometimes people do this with gifts they don't like—yikes!)

Have you ever regifted a gift?

By the way, "regifting" is actually a word. I'm serious. I've heard it before but didn't actually think it was a real word. Um, yeah!

When you think about it, regifting is all about the kingdom of God and the Lord's way of doing things.

Let me explain...

He gives us gifts so we can give them to others and bless someone else. Oh sure, we don't have to rewrap them, and we're not passing them on because we don't want them, but in God's way of doing things, He wants us to regift. To take the gift we've been given and give it to someone else for His Glory!

Way cool!

He sows these seeds in our hearts—seeds that break through the surface of our lives, grow, and bear fruit. Fruit that we give to others. Fruit that nourishes them. That takes root in their hearts, as it did in ours.

Romans 6:23 tells us, "For the wages of sin is death, but the gift of God is eternal life in Christ Jesus our Lord." And

THAT'S the best regift of all—the regift of all regifts!

And everywhere we go, God wants us to keep that one moving...especially the greatest gift of all: His Son!

Peace Out, Girl Scout...

Yeah, I was never a Girl Scout. My friends and I just say that sometimes when we say good-bye. Did I just say good-bye? Pretend I didn't, okay? The show must go on. This party we're having has to go on forever—right?

Hey, wait a minute, are you or were you ever a Girl Scout? My mom was a Brownie when she was a little girl. I think I need to ask her what that was like. And why "brownie"? Why not "candy" or "cupcake"?

Here's the deal, sista, I don't like this part at all!

(Hold on a minute—I just called you "sista," because we're, like, tight now. Oh yeah!)

So I don't like THIS PART, the dreadful moment when we have to come to the end of our hanging-out-together time. Please tell me you're with me and that you don't want this to end either. Ya know it really doesn't have to end here, does it? No, we can stay in touch and continue this journey.

How?

The **HCWG** website, of course (I'm sure you know it by now, at least you'd better—www.hotchocolatewithgod.com).

My sister, Erin, and I want to stay as connected to you as we possibly can. We're both busy with school and stuff, but if we really try I think we can do it!

Are you with me?

We're just a message away!

Ugh, I wish I had a bag of BBQ potato chips and a Japanese soda right now. Oh my goodness, I can't believe I didn't tell you about my new favorite drink. I know; I'll just show you. This will be the shortest **Cam Clip** you've ever watched. Check it out!

♪ CAM CLIPS CODE: JAPANESE SODA

Okay, I admit it, I'm trying to distract you; pretty much anything I possibly can so I don't have to say good-bye.

Don't you wish we were neighbors? Wouldn't it be so cool if we went to the same school? Seriously, I wish you were here with me right now.

Here's the deal, someday we'll be together forever. It's true! God is preparing a special place for us. Like right this very minute He is getting everything ready! And at just the right moment, in the blink of an eye, we will be with Him. Forever! Can you even imagine what it will be like? Are you ready?

Check out this **Sweet Truth**, it's awesome!

Sweet Truth

Do not let your hearts be troubled. Trust in God; trust also in me. In my

Father's house are many rooms; if it were not so, I would have told you. I am going there to prepare a place for you. And if I go and prepare a place for you, I will come back and take you to be with me that you also may be where I am. —John 14:1–3

This is crazy cool. If Jesus is preparing everything for us, you know it will be the absolute best ever!

Just a few **EXTREMELY IMPORTANT** things for you to remember before you go (please don't go...boo-hoo...that's code for I'm going to cry and miss you terribly).

- You are **LOVED**!
- You are **BEAUTIFUL**!
- YOU were made to **KNOW**, **LOVE**, and **GLORIFY GOD**!
- Purple looks smashing on you, my dear! Um, what I meant to say is: **SHINE, BE YOU**—because who you are is who God longs for you to be.
- **JESUS ROCKS!**

Wait, did I tell you that I don't want this to end?

Yes, I believe I did, at least a million times.

Okay, well...

We're here for you, girlfriend! Better yet, God is with you...always, no matter what, right now and forever!

We will be praying for you for sure, and hoping that you'll always remember the fun we had together. ☺

One more thing before you go—I'm going to pray over you what my mommy always prays over me...

May
the Lord bless and
keep you and make His face
shine down upon you and bring you
peace. May you know the love God has for you.
May you know that perfect love casts out all fear.
May the Lord bless you with the spirit of wisdom
and revelation, so you can know Him better. May
you be pure in heart, mind, and body. May you
be strong and courageous. And may you know
how much God loves you and how much
I love you too. In Jesus' Name...
Amen

You're great!
Love always and forever, until we're together for always,

Cam

P.S. Ha...and you thought I was saying good-bye. Not yet! Just one more very **SWEET** thing for you to do. ☺ Erin and I have hidden crowns throughout this book. Yes, like royal, full of jewels, the thing-you-wear-on-your-head-if-you're-a-princess-type crowns. Let's call this a crown scavenger hunt. Here's what you need to do: Start at the beginning of the book and count all the crowns.

Write your total here _____ .

NOW...watch this final **Cam Clip** to find out exactly how many crowns there are and why we decided to hide them for you.

CAM CLIPS CODE: CROWNS